AI for Fix & Flip Investing

How to Use AI to Find, Analyze, Renovate, and Sell Properties for Profit

By Joe Correa

Published by Live Stronger Faster

This book is for educational and informational purposes only. The author and publisher are not engaged in rendering legal, financial, or other professional advice. Readers should consult a qualified professional before making any financial decisions.

First Edition

Table of Contents

Introduction

AI for Fix & Flip Investing begins at the intersection of speed, intelligence, and execution in one of the most time-sensitive and opportunity-driven strategies in real estate. Fix and flip investing has always been about timing, precision, and disciplined decision-making, but in today's market, those who rely only on instinct or outdated manual methods are increasingly being outpaced by investors who understand how to integrate artificial intelligence into every phase of the deal cycle. This book is designed to introduce you to a completely new way of thinking about flipping properties—not as a purely hands-on, reactive business, but as a data-driven, AI-enhanced system where opportunities are identified faster, risks are calculated more accurately, renovation decisions are optimized, and exits are strategically planned before a property is even purchased. The goal is not just to help you flip houses, but to help you build a repeatable, scalable, and intelligent flipping system that removes guesswork and replaces it with structured, AI-supported decision-making.

At its core, fix and flip investing has always revolved around four key pillars: finding the right deal, accurately estimating repair costs, understanding market timing, and executing a profitable exit strategy. What artificial intelligence introduces into this framework is a level of clarity and efficiency that was previously impossible for individual investors working without large institutional teams. Instead of relying on scattered data sources, emotional decision-making, or rough contractor estimates, AI allows investors to process vast amounts of market information in seconds, compare renovation scenarios instantly, and evaluate potential profit margins with a level of precision that significantly reduces costly mistakes. In this new environment, success is no longer defined by who works the hardest, but by who leverages the smartest systems. This book will guide you through how to think in systems, how to structure your investing approach around AI tools, and how to transform what was once a high-risk, labor-intensive strategy into a streamlined and highly optimized investment model.

One of the most important shifts you will learn in this book is how AI changes the way deal sourcing is approached. Traditionally, finding profitable fix and flip opportunities required driving neighborhoods, analyzing listings manually, networking with wholesalers, and reacting quickly to market listings before competitors. While these methods still exist, they are no longer sufficient on their own. AI now enables investors to scan markets for undervalued properties using predictive analytics, identify distressed assets before they hit the open market, and evaluate neighborhood-level appreciation trends with real-time data modeling. Instead of relying on chance encounters or slow manual research, investors can now build automated systems that continuously feed them high-potential deals based on predefined investment criteria such as after-repair value thresholds, renovation cost ceilings, and profit margin targets. This shift dramatically increases both efficiency and deal quality, allowing investors to focus only on opportunities that meet strict profitability standards.

As we move deeper into the fix and flip process, one of the most critical components is understanding renovation costs and scope of work. Historically, this has been one of the most unpredictable and error-prone areas of investing. Underestimating repairs can completely eliminate profit margins, while overestimating can cause investors to walk away from otherwise strong deals. AI introduces a new level of accuracy into this process by analyzing comparable renovation projects, regional contractor pricing trends, material cost fluctuations, and property condition data to generate more reliable repair estimates. Instead of relying solely on subjective contractor opinions, investors can now use AI-driven estimation frameworks to cross-check bids, identify outliers, and build more structured renovation budgets. This reduces uncertainty and allows for more confident decision-making when evaluating whether a deal is worth pursuing. Another major transformation introduced in this book is the use of AI for market timing and exit strategy optimization. One of the most overlooked aspects of fix and flip investing is understanding when to sell and how pricing strategy impacts final profitability. Many investors focus heavily on acquisition and renovation but fail to strategically plan their exit, resulting in extended holding costs or missed profit opportunities. AI tools now allow investors to analyze real-time buyer demand, seasonal pricing trends, absorption rates, and comparable sales velocity to determine optimal listing windows and pricing strategies. This means that instead of guessing when the market is strong, investors can rely on data-driven insights that indicate when demand is peaking and how aggressively a property can be priced for maximum return without extended days on market. This level of precision in exit strategy planning is what separates average investors from highly successful, high-volume operators.

Throughout this book, you will also be introduced to the importance of integrating AI into project management and renovation execution workflows. Fix and flip investing is not just about buying and selling—it is about managing timelines, coordinating contractors, tracking budgets, and ensuring that projects stay on schedule. Delays in renovation projects can quickly erode profit margins due to holding costs such as mortgage payments, taxes, insurance, and utilities. AI-powered project management systems now allow investors to track renovation progress in real time, predict potential delays based on historical contractor performance, and adjust schedules dynamically to avoid costly overruns. This transforms the renovation phase from a reactive process into a proactive management system where risks are identified early and corrected before they become financial problems.

The role of tools such as ChatGPT and Buildertrend in this ecosystem is also central to how modern investors operate. ChatGPT becomes an analytical and strategic assistant capable of helping you evaluate deals, structure renovation scopes, compare investment scenarios, and even generate marketing descriptions for listed properties. Buildertrend and similar platforms provide the operational backbone for managing construction workflows, budgets, and contractor communication. When combined, these tools create a powerful ecosystem where decision-making, execution, and analysis are all connected through intelligent systems. This book will show you how to think about these tools not as isolated software, but as components of a fully integrated investment machine.

As you progress through the concepts in this introduction and the chapters that follow, you will begin to see a consistent theme: the transition from manual effort to systemized intelligence. Fix and flip investing in the past rewarded hustle, experience, and local knowledge. While those elements are still valuable, they are no longer enough on their own to stay competitive in fast-moving markets. The investors who will dominate in the coming years are those who understand how to combine traditional real estate principles with AI-driven decision systems that enhance speed, accuracy, and scalability. This book is designed to help you become one of those investors.

You will also explore how risk management is fundamentally transformed when AI is introduced into the fix and flip process. Risk in real estate is often associated with unknown variables such as unexpected repairs, market downturns, or financing challenges. AI helps reduce these unknowns by providing probabilistic insights into market behavior, property condition analysis, and financial modeling. Instead of operating in uncertainty, you begin to operate within a framework of calculated probabilities. This does not eliminate risk entirely, but it significantly reduces exposure to avoidable mistakes and improves your ability to anticipate challenges before they impact profitability.

Ultimately, this introduction sets the foundation for a new way of thinking about real estate investing. Fix and flip is no longer just a transactional strategy—it is becoming a data-driven business model powered by automation, predictive analytics, and intelligent decision systems. The investor who learns how to properly integrate AI into this process gains a significant advantage in speed, accuracy, and scalability. You are no longer limited by how many deals you can manually analyze or how many contractors you can personally manage. Instead, you begin building systems that allow you to evaluate more opportunities, make better decisions, and execute projects with greater consistency.

As you move forward through this book, you will not only learn how to use AI tools, but more importantly, you will learn how to think differently about fix and flip investing altogether. You will begin to see properties not just as physical assets, but as data points within a larger system of opportunity evaluation, cost optimization, and strategic exit planning. This shift in mindset is what ultimately allows investors to move from occasional success to consistent, repeatable profitability.

This is the beginning of a new phase in your investing journey, one where artificial intelligence becomes an integral part of how you source deals, analyze opportunities, manage renovations, and maximize returns. The strategies outlined in this book are designed to help you build not just individual profits, but a sustainable investing system that can scale over time. By the end of this book, you will understand how to combine human judgment with machine intelligence in a way that creates a powerful competitive advantage in the fix and flip market.

Chapter 1

Understanding AI in Fix & Flip Investing

Artificial intelligence is fundamentally changing how fix and flip investing operates, shifting it from a relationship-driven, intuition-based strategy into a structured, data-driven system that rewards speed, accuracy, and disciplined execution. In traditional real estate flipping, investors relied heavily on personal experience, local market knowledge, contractor relationships, and manual analysis of comparable sales. While these skills are still valuable, they are no longer sufficient on their own in a market where data moves instantly and opportunities are often identified and acted on within hours rather than days. AI introduces a new layer of intelligence into this process, allowing investors to process large amounts of market data, identify undervalued properties, estimate repair costs, and evaluate profit potential with a level of speed and consistency that was previously impossible without institutional-level resources.

At the core of AI-powered fix and flip investing is the ability to analyze patterns across massive datasets. Instead of manually reviewing listings one by one, AI tools can scan entire markets and identify properties that meet specific investment criteria such as price per square foot, neighborhood appreciation trends, days on market, and distress signals like price reductions or long listing durations. This allows investors to focus only on high-probability opportunities rather than wasting time on properties that do not meet their financial thresholds. The shift here is not just about efficiency, but about precision. AI does not get emotionally attached to properties, nor does it get influenced by hype or urgency. It evaluates deals purely based on data, which helps investors avoid emotional decision-making that often leads to overpaying or underestimating risk.

One of the most important transformations AI brings to fix and flip investing is in deal evaluation. Traditionally, investors relied on rough estimates for after-repair value (ARV), renovation costs, and potential profit margins. These estimates were often based on experience, contractor opinions, or comparable sales that may or may not reflect current market conditions. AI improves this process by pulling real-time comparable sales data, adjusting for location-specific trends, and factoring in micro-market fluctuations that are often invisible to manual analysis. This leads to more accurate ARV projections and more realistic profit expectations. Instead of guessing whether a deal will work, investors can now run structured scenarios that show potential outcomes based on different renovation levels, holding periods, and exit strategies. Renovation cost estimation is another area where

AI significantly improves decision-making. In traditional flipping, one of the biggest risks is underestimating repair costs, which can quickly eliminate projected profits. AI tools can analyze historical renovation data, regional labor costs, material pricing trends, and property condition reports to generate more reliable cost estimates. This does not replace contractors, but it provides investors with a powerful benchmarking system to validate bids and avoid overpaying for repairs. It also helps investors quickly determine whether a property is a cosmetic flip, a heavy renovation, or a potential teardown, allowing for faster and more informed acquisition decisions.

AI also plays a critical role in risk management, which is often overlooked in fix and flip investing. Risk in this business comes in many forms: market downturns, unexpected repairs, permitting delays, financing issues, and overextended holding periods. AI helps reduce uncertainty by identifying patterns in market behavior and flagging potential risks before they become financial problems. For example, if a neighborhood is showing declining absorption rates or increasing days on market, AI can signal that exit strategies may need to be adjusted. If renovation costs in a specific zip code are trending higher due to labor shortages, AI can factor that into deal analysis before an offer is made. This proactive approach to risk management allows investors to make more stable and informed decisions. Another key advantage of AI in fix and flip investing is speed. In competitive markets, the ability to analyze and act quickly is often the difference between securing a profitable deal and missing out entirely. AI dramatically reduces the time required to evaluate opportunities. Instead of spending hours running numbers manually, investors can generate full deal analyses in seconds. This allows for rapid decision-making and the ability to submit offers faster than competitors who are still relying on traditional methods. Speed, combined with accuracy, creates a powerful competitive advantage that compounds over time as investors are able to close more deals with fewer mistakes.

The integration of AI tools such as ChatGPT into the investing workflow further enhances this process by acting as an intelligent assistant for analysis, strategy, and communication. ChatGPT can help break down complex deals, simulate different investment scenarios, and even assist in writing contractor scopes of work or listing descriptions for resale properties. When combined with structured data from other platforms, it becomes a decision-support system that enhances every stage of the flipping process. Instead of replacing human decision-making, it strengthens it by providing clarity, structure, and alternative perspectives that might otherwise be missed. What makes AI particularly powerful in fix and flip investing is not just its ability to analyze data, but its ability to continuously improve decision quality over time. As more data is processed, patterns become clearer, predictions become more accurate, and investment strategies become more refined. This creates a compounding effect where each deal contributes to a smarter and more efficient system. Investors who embrace this approach are not just flipping individual properties—they are building intelligent investing systems that become more effective with each transaction.

However, it is important to understand that AI is not a replacement for real estate knowledge or experience. Instead, it is an amplification tool. Investors still need to understand market dynamics, renovation processes, financing structures, and exit strategies. What AI does is remove inefficiencies, reduce guesswork, and provide a clearer picture of each investment opportunity. The most successful investors in this new environment are those who combine human judgment with machine intelligence, using AI to enhance their decision-making rather than replace it.

As you move through this chapter, the goal is to shift your mindset from traditional fix and flip thinking to systems-based investing. Instead of looking at each deal as an isolated opportunity, you begin to see it as part of a larger data-driven process where every decision feeds into a smarter overall strategy. This approach allows you to scale more efficiently, reduce risk, and increase profitability over time.

By understanding how AI integrates into deal sourcing, analysis, renovation planning, and exit strategy development, you begin to see how the entire fix and flip process can be transformed into a streamlined system. This is the foundation of modern real estate investing, where success is no longer determined solely by effort or experience, but by the ability to leverage intelligent systems that enhance every stage of the investment cycle.

"The Deal That Changed Everything"

Marcus had been flipping houses for nearly a decade, and on paper, he looked successful. He had completed dozens of deals, built relationships with contractors, and developed a reputation in his local market as someone who could close quickly and decisively. But behind the scenes, the reality was far more stressful. Every deal felt like a gamble. Some flips made strong profits, others barely broke even, and a few had wiped out months of hard work due to unexpected repairs or shifting market conditions. Marcus relied heavily on instinct, gut feeling, and whatever data he could manually gather before making an offer. It worked—until it didn't.

One evening, after closing a deal that turned out far less profitable than expected, Marcus sat alone in the kitchen of a recently renovated property he was trying to sell. The house looked perfect. New floors, updated kitchen, modern bathrooms. But the numbers told a different story. Holding costs had eaten into profits, contractor delays had pushed timelines, and the final sale price was lower than projected. He wasn't losing money, but he was working harder than ever for smaller returns. That night, he asked himself a question he had been avoiding for years: "Is there a better way to do this?"

A few days later, Marcus was introduced to the idea of using artificial intelligence in real estate investing. At first, he dismissed it. He assumed it was just another tech trend that didn't apply to real-world investing. But curiosity got the better of him, and he decided to explore it. He started small, using AI tools to analyze a few properties he was already familiar with. Instead of manually comparing sales and estimating repairs, he watched as the system processed data in seconds, producing detailed breakdowns of ARV, renovation costs, and projected profit margins.

What surprised him most was not the speed, but the accuracy. One property he had been considering for weeks was flagged by the AI system as a high-risk investment due to declining sales velocity in the neighborhood and rising renovation costs in that zip code. Marcus had initially thought it was a great deal. Another property he had almost ignored was highlighted as a strong opportunity with stable appreciation trends and lower-than-average repair estimates. He decided to dig deeper—and for the first time, he began to trust the data more than his instincts.

Over the next several weeks, Marcus fully integrated AI into his workflow. He no longer started his day by driving neighborhoods or scrolling through listings blindly. Instead, he reviewed AI-generated deal reports that ranked properties based on profitability, risk, and market conditions. His decision-making process became faster and more structured. Instead of analyzing ten deals a week and maybe making one offer, he was now analyzing hundreds of opportunities and focusing only on the highest probability ones.

The transformation didn't stop there. Marcus began using AI to refine his renovation budgets. Instead of relying solely on contractor estimates, he compared multiple cost scenarios generated by the system. This helped him negotiate better pricing and avoid overcapitalizing on properties. He also used AI to time his exits more strategically, identifying the best listing windows based on market absorption rates and seasonal demand shifts. Slowly, his results began to change.

Within six months, Marcus noticed a clear shift. His profit margins increased, his holding times decreased, and his stress levels dropped significantly. For the first time in years, he felt like he wasn't just working harder—he was working smarter. Deals that once took days to evaluate were now analyzed in minutes. Opportunities he would have previously ignored were now becoming consistent profit generators.

One afternoon, while reviewing another AI-generated deal report, Marcus realized something important. The system wasn't replacing his experience—it was amplifying it. He still made the final decisions, still negotiated deals, and still managed contractors. But now, he was doing it with a level of clarity he had never had before. The guesswork was gone. The uncertainty was reduced. The chaos had been replaced with structure.

Marcus leaned back in his chair and looked at the numbers on the screen. This wasn't just a better way to flip houses. It was a completely different way of thinking about real estate. And for the first time in years, he wasn't just surviving in the market—he was beginning to build something scalable, predictable, and far more powerful than anything he had done before.

Chapter 2

AI Deal Sourcing and Opportunity Identification in Fix & Flip Investing

In fix and flip investing, everything begins with one critical skill: the ability to consistently find profitable deals. No amount of renovation expertise, marketing skill, or negotiation ability can compensate for poor acquisition decisions. Traditionally, deal sourcing required a combination of driving neighborhoods, monitoring MLS listings, building relationships with wholesalers, and reacting quickly when opportunities appeared. While these methods are still used today, they are no longer sufficient in a competitive, data-driven market where the best deals are often identified and claimed within hours. Artificial intelligence fundamentally changes this stage of the investing process by transforming deal sourcing from a reactive, manual activity into a proactive, automated system that continuously scans the market for high-quality opportunities based on investor-defined criteria.

AI-powered deal sourcing works by analyzing large volumes of real estate data across multiple sources simultaneously. Instead of relying on one platform or one method of discovery, AI systems aggregate information from MLS listings, public records, tax data, price reductions, days on market, ownership history, and neighborhood-level trends. This allows investors to identify properties that match specific investment filters such as below-market pricing, distressed conditions, high equity positions, or motivated seller indicators. The key advantage here is scale. While a human investor might analyze dozens of properties in a day, AI systems can evaluate thousands, filtering out low-quality opportunities and surfacing only those that meet predefined investment thresholds.

One of the most powerful applications of AI in deal sourcing is identifying motivated sellers before properties officially become obvious opportunities. Traditional investors often wait for signs such as expired listings, foreclosure notices, or visible distress. AI, however, can detect early signals of motivation by analyzing patterns such as price reductions over time, long listing durations without offers, absentee ownership, tax delinquency patterns, and changes in ownership behavior. These signals allow investors to engage sellers earlier in the process, often before competition intensifies. This creates a significant advantage, as early access to motivated sellers typically leads to better purchase prices and more flexible negotiation opportunities.

AI also improves geographic targeting, which is essential in fix and flip investing. Instead of manually researching neighborhoods, investors can use AI tools to analyze entire cities or regions and rank areas based on appreciation trends, renovation demand, rental strength, and resale velocity. This allows investors to focus their efforts on high-performing micro-markets rather than wasting time in areas with limited upside potential. Over time, AI systems can even learn from an investor's behavior, refining recommendations based on past successful deals and preferred investment styles, whether that is cosmetic flips, heavy rehabs, or entry-level starter homes.

Another major shift introduced by AI in deal sourcing is automation of outreach. Once potential deals are identified, AI systems can automatically generate and send personalized messages to property owners or leads through SMS, email, or direct mail workflows. These messages can be tailored based on property condition, ownership history, or inferred motivation level. Instead of manually contacting sellers one by one, investors can build automated pipelines that continuously engage new opportunities. This not only increases efficiency but also ensures that no potential lead is overlooked due to time constraints or human error.

Data scraping and public record analysis also play a major role in AI-driven deal sourcing. AI systems can extract valuable insights from county records, tax databases, and foreclosure filings to identify distressed assets long before they reach the market. For example, properties with unpaid taxes, multiple ownership transfers, or probate filings can be flagged as potential opportunities. This type of early detection gives investors access to off-market deals that are often more profitable due to reduced competition. Instead of competing on listed properties, investors can focus on direct-to-seller opportunities where negotiation power is significantly higher.

Another important advantage of AI in deal sourcing is speed of evaluation. In competitive markets, timing is everything. A profitable deal can be lost simply because an investor takes too long to analyze it. AI eliminates this delay by generating instant deal reports that include estimated ARV, repair cost ranges, projected profit margins, and risk assessments. This allows investors to make quick, informed decisions without sacrificing accuracy. Instead of spending hours analyzing whether a property is worth pursuing, investors can receive a structured analysis in seconds and immediately decide whether to move forward.

The integration of AI tools such as PropertyRadar and PropStream further enhances this system by providing detailed property-level data that feeds into larger analytical models. These platforms allow investors to filter properties based on equity levels, ownership duration, property type, and financial distress indicators. When combined with AI interpretation tools like ChatGPT, this data becomes even more powerful, as it can be transformed into actionable insights rather than raw information. Instead of simply seeing data points, investors begin to see opportunities ranked by profitability and strategic fit.

As investors begin to adopt AI-driven deal sourcing systems, their entire approach to real estate changes. Instead of actively searching for deals, they begin to manage systems that bring deals to them. This shift from manual effort to systemized opportunity generation is one of the most important transitions in modern investing. It allows investors to scale beyond their personal time limitations and evaluate far more opportunities than would be possible through traditional methods.

However, it is important to understand that AI does not eliminate the need for investor judgment. It enhances it. AI can identify patterns, rank opportunities, and highlight risks, but it is still up to the investor to make final decisions based on experience, strategy, and financial goals. The most successful fix and flip investors are those who learn how to combine AI-generated insights with real-world execution skills such as negotiation, contractor management, and market understanding.

Another critical concept introduced in this chapter is deal filtering precision. One of the biggest mistakes investors make is analyzing too many low-quality deals. AI solves this by allowing investors to set strict acquisition criteria such as minimum profit margins, maximum renovation budgets, or specific neighborhood requirements. This ensures that only high-quality deals enter the decision-making pipeline. Over time, this leads to better capital allocation, fewer mistakes, and more consistent returns.

As AI continues to evolve, deal sourcing will become increasingly predictive rather than reactive. Instead of simply identifying current opportunities, AI systems will begin forecasting future opportunities based on market trends, economic indicators, and behavioral patterns. This means investors will not only find deals faster—they will begin positioning themselves ahead of market movements, gaining access to opportunities before they are widely recognized.

Ultimately, this chapter establishes a new way of thinking about deal sourcing. It is no longer about searching harder or longer—it is about building intelligent systems that continuously analyze, filter, and deliver opportunities aligned with your investment strategy. Investors who master this approach will consistently outperform those who rely on traditional methods, not because they work harder, but because they operate with better information, faster execution, and more refined decision-making systems.

"The First Off-Market Signal"

Derek had been flipping houses for five years, and like most investors in his market, he believed he had a solid system. He drove neighborhoods on weekends, checked MLS listings every morning, and maintained relationships with a few wholesalers who occasionally sent him deals. Some months were good, others were inconsistent, but he accepted that as part of the business. In his mind, real estate investing was supposed to be competitive, unpredictable, and heavily dependent on timing. What he didn't realize was that his entire approach was about to be challenged.

One afternoon, while reviewing yet another batch of MLS listings, Derek noticed something unusual. A property he had been tracking for weeks had reduced its price for the third time. On paper, it still looked slightly overpriced, but something about the pattern caught his attention. The listing had been active for over 90 days. The seller had dropped the price twice before. And now it was being relisted with a new agent. Normally, Derek would have passed on it, assuming it wasn't worth the effort. But this time, he decided to test something new.

A friend had recently introduced him to an AI-driven real estate analysis tool. Skeptical but curious, Derek input the property address. Within seconds, the system generated a full report. It showed estimated after-repair value, suggested renovation costs based on similar homes in the area, and a projected profit margin range. But what caught Derek's attention wasn't just the numbers—it was the risk indicators. The system flagged the property as a "high-motivation probability listing," citing extended market time, repeated price reductions, and ownership history suggesting potential financial pressure.

Derek leaned back in his chair. He had seen hundreds of properties like this before, but he had never viewed them through this lens. The AI wasn't just giving him data—it was interpreting behavior patterns. According to the report, there was a high likelihood that the seller would accept an offer below asking price if approached quickly and directly. That insight alone changed how he viewed the deal.

Instead of waiting, Derek decided to act. The AI system automatically generated a personalized outreach message based on the property data. It wasn't generic—it referenced the listing history and expressed interest in solving a problem rather than just buying a house. Within 48 hours, the seller responded. They were frustrated with the listing process, had already considered multiple price drops, and were open to discussing a faster off-market solution. What happened next surprised Derek even more. Instead of entering a competitive bidding situation, he found himself in a direct negotiation with a motivated seller who was willing to accept a lower offer in exchange for speed and certainty. There were no bidding wars, no emotional escalation, and no wasted time. Just a straightforward conversation that led to an agreement faster than any deal he had ever closed before.

As Derek reviewed the numbers again, something clicked. The deal wasn't just profitable—it had been identified in a way he never would have done manually. Without the AI analysis, he likely would have passed on it or approached it too late. The system had identified motivation signals he had completely overlooked.

A few weeks later, Derek closed on the property. The renovation stayed within budget, and the resale price came in higher than projected. The profit margin wasn't just good—it was one of his best yet. But what stayed with him wasn't the profit. It was the process.

For the first time, Derek realized that deal sourcing didn't have to feel like searching in the dark. It could be structured, predictable, and guided by data instead of instinct alone. The

AI hadn't replaced his experience—it had expanded it. It showed him patterns he had been missing for years.

That night, as he updated his records, Derek made a decision. He wasn't going back to the old way of finding deals. From now on, he wasn't just an investor driving around hoping to find opportunities. He was building a system that brought opportunities directly to him.

Chapter 3

AI Property Analysis and Deal Evaluation in Fix & Flip Investing

Once a potential fix and flip deal has been identified, the most critical phase begins: evaluating whether the property actually makes financial sense. This is where many investors either succeed or fail. Deal analysis is not simply about estimating numbers—it is about understanding the relationship between purchase price, renovation costs, after-repair value, holding time, financing structure, and exit conditions. In traditional investing, this process is often slow, inconsistent, and heavily dependent on experience. Investors manually pull comparable sales, estimate repairs based on visual inspection, and calculate profits using spreadsheets or rough mental math. While this method can work, it leaves significant room for error. Artificial intelligence transforms this stage by introducing speed, structure, and data-driven precision into every layer of property evaluation.

AI property analysis begins with the ability to instantly process comparable sales data and generate a realistic after-repair value (ARV). Instead of manually selecting comps that may or may not be accurate, AI systems analyze a wide range of recent transactions, adjust for square footage, location proximity, condition, and market timing, and then generate a more statistically grounded valuation range. This eliminates one of the biggest risks in fix and flip investing: overestimating ARV. When ARV is inflated, every other part of the deal becomes distorted, leading to false confidence and shrinking or even eliminating profit margins. AI reduces this risk by grounding valuation in broader datasets rather than limited human-selected comparisons.

Another key component of AI-powered deal evaluation is renovation cost estimation. Traditionally, investors rely on contractor quotes, personal experience, or rough per-square-foot assumptions. These methods can vary widely depending on who provides the estimate and how detailed the scope of work is. AI introduces a more structured approach by analyzing historical renovation data, regional labor costs, material pricing trends, and property condition inputs. It can break down a property into categories such as cosmetic updates, moderate rehabilitation, or full structural renovation, and assign realistic cost ranges based on similar past projects. This helps investors quickly determine whether a deal is financially viable before investing significant time in contractor negotiations or inspections.

AI also improves the accuracy of profit margin calculations by integrating all key variables into a unified model. Instead of looking at purchase price, rehab costs, and ARV in isolation, AI evaluates the full investment lifecycle. This includes holding costs such as mortgage payments, taxes, insurance, utilities, closing costs, and potential delays in renovation or resale. By including these factors, investors get a more realistic picture of net profit rather than gross projections. This shift is critical because many investors underestimate holding costs, which can significantly reduce actual returns even when a deal appears profitable on paper.

Risk scoring is another powerful advancement in AI-driven property analysis. Every fix and flip deal carries risk, but not all risks are visible at first glance. AI systems can assign risk scores based on multiple factors including market volatility, neighborhood stability, liquidity of comparable properties, renovation complexity, and historical price fluctuations in the area. This allows investors to compare multiple deals not just based on profit potential, but also based on risk-adjusted returns. In other words, a slightly lower profit deal with lower risk may be more attractive than a high-margin deal with unpredictable variables.

One of the most valuable contributions of AI in this stage is scenario modeling. Instead of evaluating a single static outcome, investors can run multiple scenarios to understand how different variables impact profitability. For example, what happens if renovation costs increase by 15 percent? What if the property takes 60 days longer to sell? What if the ARV drops due to a market shift? AI allows investors to simulate these scenarios instantly, giving them a deeper understanding of downside risk before committing capital. This transforms decision-making from guesswork into structured analysis.

The integration of tools like DealCheck and Mashvisor enhances this process even further by providing investor-focused analytics such as cash flow projections, rental comparables, and market trend data. When combined with AI interpretation tools like ChatGPT, these platforms become part of a larger analytical system rather than standalone tools. ChatGPT can help break down complex data, explain inconsistencies, and even suggest alternative strategies such as renting instead of flipping or adjusting renovation scope to improve margins. This creates a multi-layered evaluation process where data is not only collected but actively interpreted and refined.

Speed is another major advantage of AI in property analysis. In competitive markets, deals often require immediate decisions. Waiting days to analyze a property can result in missed opportunities. AI reduces this delay by generating comprehensive deal reports in seconds. Investors can instantly see projected profits, risk levels, and recommended action steps. This allows for faster decision-making without sacrificing accuracy, which is essential in fix and flip investing where timing directly impacts profitability.

AI also introduces consistency into deal evaluation. One of the biggest challenges for investors is inconsistency in analysis. A deal might be evaluated differently depending on mood, time constraints, or external pressure. AI eliminates this variability by applying the same structured logic to every property. This ensures that every deal is evaluated using the same financial standards, reducing emotional bias and improving long-term decision quality.

Another important concept is capital efficiency. AI helps investors understand not just whether a deal is profitable, but how efficiently capital is being used. Two deals may generate similar profits, but one may require significantly more capital or carry longer holding periods. AI helps highlight these differences by comparing return on investment (ROI), internal rate of return (IRR), and capital turnover speed. This allows investors to prioritize deals that generate faster and more efficient returns, rather than simply chasing the highest dollar profit.

As investors continue to use AI in deal analysis, they begin to shift their mindset from individual property evaluation to portfolio thinking. Instead of asking "Is this deal good?" they begin asking "How does this deal fit into my overall investment strategy?" AI supports this shift by allowing investors to compare multiple deals side by side and understand how each one impacts overall portfolio performance. This creates a more strategic approach to investing where decisions are made based on long-term goals rather than short-term opportunities.

Ultimately, AI property analysis is about reducing uncertainty and increasing clarity. It does not eliminate risk, but it helps investors understand risk more deeply and make more informed decisions. By combining data-driven insights with human judgment, investors gain a powerful advantage in identifying which deals are worth pursuing and which should be avoided.

This chapter establishes a critical foundation in fix and flip investing: the ability to evaluate deals with precision, speed, and confidence. Investors who master AI-driven analysis are no longer guessing—they are making structured, informed decisions based on real data and scenario modeling. This shift dramatically improves consistency, reduces costly mistakes, and increases overall profitability.

"The Deal Everyone Misjudged"

Samantha had been flipping houses for nearly six years, and she prided herself on being conservative with her numbers. Unlike many investors in her market, she rarely overpaid and always tried to build in extra cushion for repairs and holding costs. Still, her results were inconsistent. Some deals performed extremely well, while others barely broke even despite careful planning. She couldn't understand why her results varied so much when she felt like she was doing everything correctly.

One day, she came across a property that looked like a perfect flip. It was in a desirable neighborhood, had strong comparable sales nearby, and was listed below what she believed was market value. The house needed cosmetic updates—new flooring, kitchen upgrades, paint, and minor repairs. On paper, it looked like an easy win. Her initial analysis showed a solid profit margin, and she quickly ran the numbers again to confirm. Everything seemed to align.

However, before making an offer, Samantha decided to test something new. A colleague had introduced her to an AI-based property analysis system, and although she was skeptical, she decided to input the deal details. Within seconds, the system generated a full breakdown. At first, the results looked similar to her own analysis. But then she noticed something unexpected. The AI flagged the renovation costs as significantly higher than her estimate. It broke down the property condition into categories she had not fully considered, including hidden electrical issues, potential plumbing updates based on the age of the home, and regional labor cost increases that had occurred over the past six months. It also adjusted the ARV downward slightly based on more recent comparable sales that reflected a cooling trend in the neighborhood.

Samantha frowned. She double-checked her own numbers. She had not included those additional repair categories, and she had relied on comps that were slightly older than the ones the AI system used. For the first time, she began to question her initial confidence in the deal.

Curious, she ran a second scenario in the AI system, adjusting for potential delays in renovation and a slower-than-expected resale timeline. The projected profit margin dropped significantly. What had initially looked like a strong deal now appeared borderline at best. Samantha felt a mix of frustration and curiosity. If she had relied only on her own analysis, she likely would have moved forward with the purchase.

Instead of walking away immediately, she decided to dig deeper. She contacted her contractor for a second opinion, specifically asking about the issues highlighted by the AI. To her surprise, the contractor confirmed several of the concerns. The electrical system was outdated, plumbing updates were likely needed, and material costs had increased more than she realized. The contractor's revised estimate matched closely with the AI-generated projection.

Samantha sat quietly after the call. The realization was unsettling but clear. She had almost made a decision based on incomplete information. Not because she was inexperienced, but because no single person can accurately process every variable in real time. The AI had not replaced her judgment—it had expanded it.

She decided not to move forward with the deal.

Two weeks later, she reviewed another property. This time, she approached it differently. Instead of trusting her initial analysis alone, she ran it through the AI system first. The results were surprisingly different from what she expected. The property she thought was average was actually flagged as a high-opportunity deal with strong upside potential due to underestimated ARV growth and lower-than-expected renovation complexity.

She moved forward with confidence, structured her offer based on the AI analysis, and secured the property below asking price. The renovation went smoothly, and the resale came in higher than projected. For the first time, Samantha felt like she wasn't just guessing anymore. She was operating with clarity.

Months later, she looked back at the first deal she had almost purchased. It had sold—but for far less profit than she originally estimated. Seeing that confirmed everything she had learned.

She realized something important that day. In real estate investing, the biggest risk wasn't missing out on deals—it was misjudging them. And now, she finally had a way to see more clearly than ever before.

Chapter 4

AI Exit Strategy Optimization and Profit Maximization in Fix & Flip Investing

In fix and flip investing, the exit strategy is where all prior decisions are ultimately tested. You can acquire the right property, estimate repairs accurately, and manage renovations effectively, but if your exit is poorly timed or incorrectly priced, your profits can quickly shrink or disappear entirely. Traditional investors often focus heavily on acquisition and renovation but treat the exit as a final step rather than a strategic phase. This is one of the most common mistakes in flipping houses. Artificial intelligence changes this by transforming the exit strategy into a data-driven, predictive process that begins long before the property is ever listed for sale.

AI exit strategy optimization starts with understanding real-time market absorption. Absorption rate refers to how quickly homes are selling in a specific market or submarket. In traditional investing, many investors rely on general market sentiment or outdated comparables when deciding when to list a property. AI systems, however, continuously track how long similar properties are staying on the market, how often price reductions are occurring, and how buyer demand is shifting week by week. This allows investors to identify optimal listing windows when demand is strongest and competition is weakest, increasing the probability of faster sales and higher offers.

Another key component of AI-driven exit strategy is dynamic pricing optimization. Pricing a flipped property correctly is one of the most important decisions in the entire investment cycle. If a property is priced too high, it may sit on the market, increasing holding costs and reducing profit margins. If it is priced too low, money is left on the table. AI tools analyze comparable listings in real time, adjust for condition, location, and market velocity, and generate pricing recommendations that balance speed of sale with maximum profitability. Instead of relying on static pricing strategies, investors can now adjust pricing dynamically based on live market feedback.

AI also enhances understanding of buyer behavior patterns, which is critical for successful exits. Different markets attract different types of buyers, such as first-time homeowners, investors, or move-up buyers. AI systems can analyze demographic data, financing trends, and historical buyer behavior to determine who is most likely to purchase a specific property type. This allows investors to tailor marketing strategies, staging decisions, and even renovation choices to align with the preferences of the most likely buyer pool. When a property is aligned with buyer expectations, it sells faster and at stronger prices.

Timing is another area where AI significantly improves exit outcomes. Seasonal trends, interest rate changes, and local economic conditions all influence when buyers are most active. Traditionally, investors might rely on general knowledge such as "spring is a good time to sell," but AI provides far more precise insights. It can identify micro-trends such as weekly demand fluctuations, shifts in mortgage applications, and regional inventory levels. This allows investors to time listings more strategically rather than relying on broad assumptions. Even a few weeks of timing optimization can significantly impact final profit margins.

AI also plays a major role in reducing holding costs through predictive planning. Holding costs such as mortgage payments, utilities, taxes, insurance, and maintenance expenses accumulate over time and directly reduce profitability. AI systems can forecast expected days on market based on current pricing strategy and market conditions, allowing investors to estimate total holding costs before listing. This enables better decision-making regarding pricing adjustments, renovation completion timing, and even whether to sell or rent the property if market conditions shift unexpectedly. Another powerful aspect of AI exit optimization is scenario-based exit modeling. Instead of assuming a single selling outcome, investors can run multiple exit scenarios. For example, what happens if the property sells within 15 days at a slightly lower price? What if it takes 60 days but sells at full asking price? What if the market slows and requires a price adjustment? AI systems model these scenarios in advance, giving investors a clearer understanding of risk versus reward. This helps prevent emotional decision-making during the listing process, especially when properties are not selling as quickly as expected.

Marketing optimization is another critical layer in AI-driven exits. Traditional flipping relies heavily on listing photos, MLS exposure, and basic online marketing. AI enhances this by analyzing which listing descriptions, images, and staging styles generate the highest engagement in specific markets. It can even recommend optimal photo sequences, highlight features that attract buyers, and generate listing descriptions tailored to buyer psychology. When combined with platforms like Zillow or MLS syndication tools, this creates a highly optimized marketing engine that increases visibility and buyer interest.

AI tools also help investors decide between different exit strategies, such as selling retail, selling to investors, or holding the property as a rental. Instead of defaulting to a single strategy, AI can compare projected returns across multiple exit paths. For example, a property might generate a moderate profit if sold immediately, but significantly higher long-term returns if refinanced and converted into a rental. By comparing these scenarios, investors can make more strategic decisions based on capital goals, risk tolerance, and market conditions.

One of the most important shifts introduced by AI in exit strategy is the concept of real-time adjustment. In traditional investing, once a property is listed, many investors remain passive unless significant issues arise. AI allows for continuous monitoring of listing performance. If a property is receiving low engagement, the system can recommend price adjustments, marketing changes, or even repositioning strategies. This proactive approach ensures that properties do not stagnate on the market, which is one of the biggest threats to flip profitability.

Ultimately, AI exit strategy optimization transforms the final phase of fix and flip investing from a reactive process into a proactive, continuously optimized system. Instead of guessing when and how to sell, investors operate with real-time data, predictive modeling, and structured decision frameworks. This leads to faster sales, higher profits, and more consistent investment outcomes.

When combined with deal sourcing, property analysis, and renovation planning, AI-driven exit optimization completes the full lifecycle of intelligent fix and flip investing. Each phase feeds into the next, creating a connected system where every decision is informed by data rather than intuition alone. Investors who master this integrated approach gain a significant advantage in efficiency, profitability, and scalability.

"The Listing That Almost Stalled"

Jordan had built a solid reputation as a fix and flip investor in his area. He wasn't the biggest player, but he was consistent. He knew how to find decent deals, manage renovations, and get properties listed quickly. Over time, he developed a rhythm: buy, renovate, list, sell, repeat. Most of his projects followed a similar pattern, and for a while, everything worked smoothly. But one particular deal changed how he thought about everything that came after the renovation.

The property was a small three-bedroom home in a growing suburban neighborhood. Jordan had acquired it below market value, completed a light renovation, and transformed it into a modern, attractive home. New floors, updated kitchen, fresh paint, and improved landscaping made it one of the nicest homes on the block. Based on his initial estimates, he expected a strong and relatively quick sale.

When the renovation was complete, Jordan listed the property at what he believed was a competitive price. The first few days went well. Showings were scheduled, and interest seemed strong. But after the first week, activity slowed. Then the second week passed with only a handful of inquiries. By the third week, the listing had gone quiet. No offers. No serious buyers. Just occasional views and lukewarm feedback.

Frustrated, Jordan reviewed his pricing strategy. He compared recent sales and confirmed that his listing price was aligned with similar properties. Everything appeared correct on paper, yet the market response didn't match his expectations. That's when he decided to try something different.

A colleague had recently shown him an AI-driven real estate optimization tool, and although Jordan had used it briefly for deal analysis, he had never applied it to an active listing. He input the property details, listing history, and current pricing strategy. Within moments, the system generated an exit performance report.

What he saw surprised him.

The AI indicated that while the pricing was technically within market range, buyer engagement data suggested the property was misaligned with the current demand cycle. The system showed that similar homes were receiving higher engagement at slightly lower price points, and that buyer activity in the area had shifted toward more aggressively priced listings due to rising interest rates. Even more interesting was the timing analysis. The AI showed that the strongest buyer activity window for that neighborhood had occurred two weeks earlier. Jordan had listed just after the peak demand period had passed. The system also suggested that homes with similar features were now sitting slightly longer unless priced more competitively.

Jordan felt a sinking feeling in his stomach. He had done everything "right," but he had missed the timing window entirely.

The AI then generated three potential exit scenarios. The first was to reduce the price slightly and relaunch immediately to capture remaining demand. The second was to hold and wait for a potential market rebound, though this came with increased holding costs and uncertainty. The third was to reposition the listing with updated marketing and a targeted pricing adjustment designed to re-enter buyer attention cycles.

For the first time, Jordan realized he wasn't just choosing between price adjustments—he was choosing between strategic outcomes.

He decided to follow the AI recommendation and adjust the

pricing slightly while updating the listing description and visuals. The system even suggested changes in how the home's features should be highlighted, focusing more on lifestyle benefits rather than renovation details.

Within days, everything changed.

Showings increased. Buyer interest returned. And within ten days, an offer came in—stronger than he expected after the slow period. The property sold shortly after, with only a minor reduction in profit compared to his original expectation.

After closing, Jordan reviewed the entire process again. What stood out to him was not just the recovery, but how close he had come to letting the property sit too long on the market. Without the AI insights, he likely would have waited longer, hoping the market would respond on its own.

Instead, he had learned something critical: timing the exit was not just about listing a property—it was about continuously understanding how the market was reacting in real time.

From that moment forward, Jordan stopped thinking of exits as a final step. He began treating them as a living strategy—one that required constant monitoring, adjustment, and data-driven decisions.

And for the first time, his flips didn't just sell—they performed exactly the way he planned them to.

Chapter 5

AI Project Management and Renovation Execution in Fix & Flip Investing

In fix and flip investing, the renovation phase is where many deals succeed or fail in real terms. Even when a property is purchased correctly and analyzed properly, poor execution during renovation can destroy profit margins. Delays, budget overruns, contractor mismanagement, and scope creep are some of the most common issues investors face. Traditionally, managing renovations has relied heavily on personal oversight, contractor communication, handwritten budgets, and reactive problem-solving. This approach works in small volumes but becomes extremely difficult to scale or control as multiple projects run simultaneously. Artificial intelligence introduces a new way to manage renovations by turning project execution into a structured, monitored, and predictive system.

AI project management begins with structured renovation planning. Before any work starts, AI systems can break down a property into detailed renovation phases, including demolition, structural work, mechanical systems, interior finishes, and final staging preparation. Each phase can be assigned estimated timelines, cost ranges, and dependency relationships. This creates a full project roadmap that outlines not just what needs to be done, but when and in what order. Instead of relying on rough contractor estimates, investors can now visualize the entire renovation process as a structured workflow with clearly defined milestones.

One of the most powerful applications of AI in renovation execution is cost control. Renovation budgets often fail because initial estimates are too optimistic or incomplete. AI systems help solve this by analyzing historical renovation data from similar properties, regional cost trends, and material pricing fluctuations. This allows for more realistic budget forecasting before work begins. As the project progresses, AI can continuously compare actual spending against projected budgets and flag deviations early. This real-time financial tracking helps investors identify cost overruns before they become critical problems.

Another critical area where AI improves renovation management is timeline prediction. In traditional flipping, delays are common due to contractor availability, material shortages, permit issues, or unexpected structural problems. These delays can significantly increase holding costs and reduce overall profitability. AI systems can analyze historical contractor performance, regional construction timelines, and project complexity to predict potential delays before they occur. If a contractor typically runs behind schedule on similar projects, the system can flag this risk early, allowing the investor to adjust expectations or take corrective action.

AI also improves contractor coordination and communication. In many renovation projects, miscommunication between investors and contractors leads to errors, rework, and wasted time. AI-powered project management tools can centralize communication, track task completion, and ensure that all stakeholders are aligned on scope and expectations. Instead of relying on scattered text messages or verbal updates, investors can view structured dashboards that show project progress in real time. This improves accountability and reduces the likelihood of misunderstandings that lead to costly mistakes.

Scope management is another area where AI adds significant value. One of the most common issues in fix and flip projects is scope creep, where additional work is added during renovation without proper cost or timeline adjustments. AI systems can help define a clear initial scope and flag any deviations from the original plan. If a contractor suggests additional work, the system can immediately evaluate how that change impacts budget, timeline, and projected profit margin. This allows investors to make informed decisions rather than emotional or reactive approvals. Material procurement and supply chain management also benefit from AI integration. Delays in material delivery can halt entire projects, leading to extended holding costs. AI systems can track material availability, predict potential shortages, and recommend alternative suppliers when needed. By anticipating supply chain disruptions, investors can reduce downtime and keep projects moving forward efficiently. This level of foresight is especially important in larger renovations where multiple materials and suppliers are involved.

Another important feature of AI-driven renovation management is progress tracking through data inputs. Instead of physically visiting a property to assess progress, investors can receive structured updates that include photos, budget updates, and milestone completions. AI systems can even analyze visual data from job site photos to estimate completion percentage and identify inconsistencies or incomplete work. This reduces the need for constant physical oversight while still maintaining control over project quality.

Risk management is also significantly improved through AI-powered renovation systems. Renovation risk can come from many sources, including hidden structural issues, permit delays, contractor reliability, or unforeseen repair needs. AI systems can assign risk levels to each phase of the renovation based on property type, location, and contractor history. If risk levels increase during the project, investors are alerted early so they can adjust timelines or budgets accordingly. This proactive approach reduces surprises and improves overall project stability.

AI also enhances decision-making during renovation when unexpected issues arise. In traditional investing, unexpected problems often lead to rushed decisions, such as overpaying for repairs or extending timelines without proper analysis. With AI support, investors can instantly evaluate the financial impact of different solutions. For example, if a plumbing issue is discovered, the system can compare repair costs, timeline impacts, and resale value implications of different repair options. This allows for more strategic decision-making under pressure.

Another major advantage of AI in renovation execution is scalability. Managing one flip manually is challenging but manageable. Managing multiple flips simultaneously becomes significantly more complex. AI allows investors to oversee multiple projects at once without losing visibility or control. Each project can be tracked individually while still contributing to a broader portfolio-level view of performance, budget allocation, and timeline efficiency. This makes it possible for investors to scale from single-property flips to multi-project operations without a proportional increase in workload. AI also supports post-renovation analysis, which is often overlooked but extremely valuable. After a project is completed, AI can compare projected outcomes with actual results, identifying where estimates were accurate and where deviations occurred. This feedback loop allows investors to refine future renovation estimates, improve contractor selection, and enhance budgeting accuracy over time. Each project becomes a learning opportunity that improves future performance.

Ultimately, AI project management transforms renovation from a reactive, chaotic process into a structured, controlled system. Instead of constantly reacting to problems, investors begin to anticipate them. Instead of relying on memory and manual tracking, they operate through data-driven dashboards and predictive insights. This shift dramatically improves efficiency, reduces risk, and increases profitability in fix and flip investing.

As investors adopt these systems, they begin to realize that successful flipping is not just about finding and buying the right property—it is about executing the renovation process with precision, discipline, and control. AI does not replace the need for contractors or hands-on management, but it ensures that every decision is informed, every risk is visible, and every phase of the project is optimized for success.

"The Project That Almost Went Off Track"

Ethan had always considered himself a strong operator in fix and flip investing. He was organized, detail-oriented, and careful with his numbers. Over the years, he had built a reliable network of contractors and developed a system for managing renovations that worked well enough when he was handling one or two projects at a time. But everything changed when he decided to scale.

It started with a simple goal: complete three flips simultaneously. He had done multiple projects before, but never at the same time. The first few weeks went smoothly. Demolition began on schedule, materials were ordered, and contractors were aligned. Ethan felt confident that his system could handle the increased workload.

But soon, small issues began to appear.

One contractor delayed framing work by a week due to scheduling conflicts. Another project ran into unexpected plumbing issues that weren't initially identified. Material deliveries were pushed back due to supply shortages. At first, these problems seemed manageable. But as they stacked up, Ethan found himself spending more time reacting to issues than managing progress. Every day felt like damage control. He was constantly texting contractors, adjusting timelines, and recalculating budgets. Instead of focusing on strategy, he was buried in operational chaos. The stress began to build as holding costs increased and timelines extended beyond initial projections.

One evening, after reviewing all three projects, Ethan realized something unsettling. He had no clear, real-time visibility into where each renovation truly stood financially or operationally. Everything was fragmented—messages in one place, spreadsheets in another, and verbal updates that didn't always match reality.

That's when he decided to try something new.

He had recently been introduced to an AI-powered renovation management system. Skeptical but desperate for clarity, he uploaded all three project details into the platform. Within minutes, the system generated full project dashboards for each property.

What he saw immediately changed his perspective.

Each project was broken down into phases with clear progress tracking. Budget usage was compared against projections. Timeline risks were highlighted in color-coded alerts. One project was flagged as "high delay risk" due to contractor performance patterns. Another showed potential budget overrun if material costs continued trending upward.

For the first time, Ethan wasn't guessing. He was seeing everything clearly.

The system also provided recommendations. For one project, it suggested reallocating certain tasks to a different contractor with better historical performance data. For another, it recommended adjusting the renovation sequence to prevent delays in critical path items. It even suggested ordering materials earlier for the third project to avoid known supply chain delays in the region.

At first, Ethan felt overwhelmed by the amount of information. But as he studied the dashboards more closely, something clicked. This wasn't just reporting—it was guidance.

He followed the recommendations.

Within days, he began restructuring his communication process with contractors. Instead of scattered messages, everything was centralized through structured updates. He began receiving daily progress snapshots without needing to physically visit each site. Budget alerts helped him catch overspending early. Timeline adjustments were made proactively rather than reactively.

Slowly, the chaos started to settle.

One of the projects, which had been falling behind schedule, stabilized after contractor adjustments were made. Another project came back under budget after early material procurement. Even the most problematic renovation began moving forward more smoothly once scope clarity was enforced through the system.

A few weeks later, Ethan stood inside one of the completed properties. The renovation had finished slightly later than originally planned, but far more efficiently than he had feared during the peak of the issues. The budget had stayed within acceptable range, and the quality of work was strong.

As he walked through the finished home, he realized something important.

The problem had never been his contractors alone. It had been his lack of visibility and control.

Without structured systems, he had been managing chaos manually. With AI, he was finally managing data, not confusion.

Later that night, Ethan reviewed all three projects again. This time, he wasn't stressed. He was analyzing. Learning. Improving.

For the first time since scaling his business, he felt something different—not pressure, but control.

And he understood something clearly: in fix and flip investing, success wasn't just about finding deals or managing renovations. It was about building systems that allowed you to see everything clearly enough to make the right decisions before problems became costly mistakes.

Chapter 6

AI Scaling Systems and Portfolio Expansion in Fix & Flip Investing

As investors gain experience in fix and flip investing, a natural progression occurs: the desire to move from individual deals to a scalable system. Most investors begin by focusing on one property at a time, carefully managing each phase of the process. However, true wealth creation in real estate does not come from isolated transactions—it comes from systems that allow consistent, repeatable execution across multiple properties simultaneously. Artificial intelligence is the key factor that enables this transition. It transforms fix and flip investing from a hands-on job into a structured, scalable business model capable of operating at portfolio level rather than deal level.

Scaling in traditional fix and flip investing is difficult because it requires increased time, attention, and coordination. Each additional project adds complexity: more contractors, more budgets, more timelines, and more opportunities for errors. Without systems in place, scaling often leads to burnout or declining performance. AI changes this equation by introducing automation, structure, and predictive control across multiple projects. Instead of manually managing every detail, investors can rely on AI systems to monitor performance, track progress, and highlight issues before they become critical.

At the foundation of AI scaling is centralized data management. In a traditional setup, each property is often tracked separately using spreadsheets, notes, or disconnected tools. This creates fragmentation, making it difficult to see overall performance across multiple deals. AI solves this by consolidating all property data into a single integrated dashboard. Investors can view acquisition costs, renovation budgets, timelines, projected profits, and risk levels for every property in their portfolio simultaneously. This creates a unified system where decisions are based on portfolio-wide insights rather than isolated project snapshots.

Another critical component of scaling is automation of repetitive tasks. In fix and flip investing, many activities are repetitive but necessary, such as lead follow-ups, contractor updates, budget tracking, and progress reporting. AI systems can automate many of these tasks, reducing manual workload while increasing consistency. For example, automated alerts can notify investors when budgets exceed thresholds, when renovation milestones are delayed, or when market conditions change in ways that impact exit strategies. This allows investors to focus on decision-making rather than administrative tasks. AI also enhances scalability by improving capital allocation decisions. As investors begin managing multiple projects, one of the biggest challenges is determining where to allocate time, money, and attention. Not all deals perform equally, and some require more resources than others. AI helps rank properties based on projected ROI, risk levels, and capital efficiency. This allows investors to prioritize high-performing assets and make informed decisions about where to deploy additional resources. Instead of treating all deals equally, investors begin managing their portfolio strategically based on data-driven prioritization.

Another major advantage of AI in scaling is performance forecasting. Traditional investors often rely on intuition or past experience to predict outcomes. AI, however, uses historical data, market trends, and real-time project inputs to forecast future performance across multiple properties. This includes projected profit margins, expected timelines, and risk-adjusted returns. By understanding future outcomes in advance, investors can make proactive adjustments to improve results across their entire portfolio.

AI also plays a key role in identifying bottlenecks within a scaling operation. As the number of projects increases, inefficiencies naturally emerge. These may include contractor delays, inconsistent renovation costs, or slow deal analysis processes. AI systems can detect these bottlenecks by analyzing performance patterns across multiple projects. Once identified, the system can recommend solutions such as reallocating contractors, adjusting timelines, or modifying acquisition criteria. This ensures that scaling does not lead to inefficiency, but instead leads to continuous optimization.

Another important concept in AI scaling is portfolio balancing. A well-structured fix and flip portfolio should not rely too heavily on one type of deal or market segment. AI helps investors balance their portfolio by analyzing exposure across different property types, neighborhoods, risk levels, and investment strategies. For example, an investor might unknowingly concentrate too many high-risk renovations in one market. AI systems can identify this imbalance and recommend diversification strategies to reduce exposure and stabilize returns.

AI also improves decision-making speed at scale. When managing multiple properties, delays in decision-making can create ripple effects across the entire portfolio. AI reduces this friction by providing instant analysis for new opportunities, renovation adjustments, and exit strategies. This allows investors to maintain momentum even as complexity increases. Instead of slowing down as they scale, investors can maintain or even increase operational speed. Another powerful feature of AI-driven scaling is predictive deal flow management. Instead of constantly searching for new deals manually, investors can build systems that continuously feed them opportunities based on predefined criteria. AI can filter leads, rank opportunities, and prioritize deals based on portfolio needs. For example, if an investor needs faster-turnaround flips to balance cash flow, AI can prioritize properties that meet those criteria. This ensures that deal flow is aligned with strategic goals rather than random availability.

Risk distribution is another area where AI enhances scaling. As portfolios grow, exposure to risk increases. AI helps manage this by evaluating risk at both the individual property level and the portfolio level. It can identify correlations between deals, highlight overexposure to certain markets, and suggest adjustments to reduce overall risk concentration. This creates a more stable and resilient investment structure capable of withstanding market fluctuations.

AI also improves long-term strategy development. Instead of focusing only on individual flips, investors begin thinking in terms of cycles and systems. AI helps model long-term outcomes based on different scaling strategies. For example, what happens if an investor completes five flips per year versus fifteen? How does reinvesting profits into larger deals impact long-term wealth creation? These strategic insights allow investors to move beyond short-term gains and build long-term investment systems. Perhaps one of the most important transformations AI brings to scaling is the shift from operator to system owner. In traditional fix and flip investing, the investor is deeply involved in every detail. In AI-supported systems, the investor becomes more of a manager of systems rather than a direct operator of tasks. This shift frees up time, reduces stress, and allows for broader strategic thinking. Instead of being limited by personal bandwidth, investors are limited only by the capacity of their systems.

Ultimately, AI scaling systems redefine what is possible in fix and flip investing. What once required full-time hands-on involvement can now be managed through structured systems that handle analysis, monitoring, forecasting, and optimization. This does not remove the need for human judgment, but it significantly amplifies it. Investors who embrace this approach are able to grow beyond traditional limitations and build real estate businesses that operate with consistency, efficiency, and scalability.

This chapter marks a turning point in the series. It shifts the focus from individual deal execution to system-wide performance. Investors are no longer just flipping houses—they are building intelligent investment ecosystems designed to grow, adapt, and scale over time. The difference between small-scale success and long-term wealth creation lies in this transition from manual investing to AI-driven systems thinking.

"The Day He Stopped Working Inside the System"

Caleb had always considered himself a hardworking investor. He was involved in every detail of his fix and flip projects. From the moment he acquired a property to the day it sold, he stayed hands-on. He reviewed contractor bids, tracked renovation progress, managed budgets, and personally oversaw every decision. For years, this approach worked. He made consistent profits, learned the business deeply, and built a solid reputation in his local market.

But as time went on, Caleb began to feel something changing.

He wasn't scaling.

He was repeating.

Each new deal felt like starting over. The same decisions. The same problems. The same stress. Even though he was making money, he realized his income was tied directly to his time and attention. If he stopped working, everything slowed down. If he got overwhelmed, deals stalled. If multiple projects overlapped, he felt stretched thin.

One afternoon, while reviewing three active flips at once, Caleb realized he was spending more time managing problems than making strategic decisions. One contractor was behind schedule. Another project had budget overruns. A third needed immediate attention because inspections revealed unexpected issues. His phone kept buzzing with updates, questions, and urgent decisions.

He leaned back in his chair and asked himself a simple question.

"If I keep scaling like this, what happens when I reach ten projects?"

The answer wasn't comforting.

That's when he was introduced to an AI-driven real estate scaling system. At first, he didn't believe it could handle real renovation work. He assumed it was just reporting software or basic automation. But curiosity pushed him to test it.

He uploaded data from his current portfolio into the system.

Within minutes, everything changed.

Instead of three separate chaotic projects, Caleb saw a unified dashboard. All properties were displayed together with real-time updates on budget usage, renovation progress, risk levels, and projected profits. For the first time, he wasn't looking at scattered information—he was looking at a complete system. One property was flagged as high risk due to contractor delays. Another was performing better than expected, with higher projected margins. The third was slightly over budget but still within acceptable profit range. The system didn't just show problems—it ranked priorities.

Caleb felt something unfamiliar: clarity.

Over the next few days, he began following the system's recommendations. It suggested reallocating contractor resources between projects. It recommended delaying non-critical work on one property to protect cash flow. It even predicted that one flip should be listed two weeks earlier than planned to avoid market slowdown risks.

At first, Caleb resisted. He was used to making all decisions himself. But slowly, he started trusting the patterns.

And things began to improve.

Delays were reduced. Communication became more structured. Budget overruns decreased. Instead of reacting to problems, Caleb started preventing them. The system didn't eliminate his role—it changed it.

He was no longer inside every detail.

He was above them. One evening, he reviewed his entire portfolio again. This time, he wasn't stressed. He wasn't chasing updates or solving emergencies. He was analyzing performance like a business owner instead of a project manager.

And that's when it hit him.

He wasn't just flipping houses anymore.

He was running a system that flipped houses.

A few months later, Caleb made a decision that changed everything. He expanded to more projects—not by working harder, but by trusting the system to manage complexity. What once felt impossible now felt structured. Predictable. Scalable.

For the first time in his investing career, Caleb wasn't limited by his time.

He was limited only by how far his system could grow.

And now, there was no ceiling at all.

Chapter 7

AI for Short-Term Rental (Airbnb) Investing in Fix & Flip Systems

Short-term rental investing, particularly through platforms like Airbnb-style properties, has become one of the most dynamic and data-sensitive segments of real estate. Unlike traditional long-term rentals or fix and flip projects, short-term rentals operate in a constantly changing environment driven by seasonality, pricing volatility, local demand shifts, and guest behavior patterns. In this space, small changes in pricing strategy, occupancy rates, or property presentation can have a significant impact on profitability. Artificial intelligence introduces a powerful advantage by turning what was once a highly reactive and uncertain strategy into a structured, predictive, and optimized system. For investors who already understand fix and flip investing, short-term rentals represent an additional layer of opportunity where AI becomes even more essential due to the speed and variability of market conditions.

AI in short-term rental investing begins with deal identification. Not every property is suitable for Airbnb-style income, and choosing the wrong property can lead to inconsistent occupancy and poor returns. Traditionally, investors relied on general assumptions about tourism demand or anecdotal market knowledge. AI systems, however, analyze large datasets including nightly rates, occupancy history, seasonal demand fluctuations, local regulations, and competitor performance. This allows investors to identify properties with strong short-term rental potential before purchase. Instead of guessing whether a location will perform well, investors can now rely on data-driven projections that estimate revenue potential with far greater accuracy.

Once a property is identified, AI plays a critical role in revenue forecasting. Unlike long-term rentals that rely on fixed monthly income, short-term rental income fluctuates daily. AI systems analyze historical booking data, local event schedules, tourism trends, and competitor pricing to generate dynamic income projections. This includes estimating average nightly rates, occupancy percentages, and seasonal highs and lows. By modeling income variability, investors can better understand real cash flow potential rather than relying on overly optimistic averages. This level of forecasting helps prevent overleveraging and improves investment stability.

Pricing optimization is one of the most powerful applications of AI in Airbnb-style investing. In traditional approaches, many investors set fixed nightly rates or adjust prices manually based on intuition. AI changes this entirely by implementing dynamic pricing models that adjust in real time based on demand conditions. If local occupancy rates rise, pricing increases automatically. If demand slows, prices adjust downward to maintain booking momentum. This ensures that properties are always competitively priced without sacrificing revenue potential. Over time, even small pricing optimizations can significantly increase annual income.

AI also enhances occupancy forecasting, which is critical for understanding overall performance. Instead of reacting to low booking periods after they occur, AI systems can predict occupancy trends weeks or months in advance. This allows investors to proactively adjust pricing, marketing strategies, or even property presentation to improve booking performance. For example, if a slow season is predicted, investors can implement targeted promotions or adjust minimum stay requirements to maintain cash flow stability.

Another important area where AI transforms short-term rental investing is guest segmentation and behavior analysis. Not all guests behave the same way, and understanding guest patterns can significantly improve both revenue and operational efficiency. AI can analyze booking sources, guest demographics, length of stay, and review patterns to identify high-value guest segments. This allows investors to tailor their listings, pricing, and amenities to attract more profitable guests. For example, business travelers may prefer different amenities than vacation families, and AI helps identify these patterns automatically.

AI also plays a major role in listing optimization. The way a property is presented online has a direct impact on booking performance. AI systems can analyze listing photos, descriptions, titles, and engagement metrics to determine what drives higher conversion rates. It can recommend improvements such as better photo sequencing, keyword optimization, and description enhancements that align with search behavior on booking platforms. This improves visibility and increases the likelihood of consistent bookings.

Operational automation is another critical advantage of AI in short-term rental systems. Managing guest communication, check-ins, cleaning schedules, and maintenance requests can become overwhelming as portfolio size increases. AI-powered automation tools can handle guest messaging, send booking confirmations, coordinate cleaning schedules, and even manage dynamic pricing updates. This reduces the need for constant manual involvement and allows investors to scale their short-term rental portfolios more efficiently.

AI also improves risk management in short-term rental investing. Risks include regulatory changes, seasonal demand drops, increased competition, and unexpected maintenance costs. AI systems can monitor local regulations, track market saturation, and identify shifts in demand patterns that could impact profitability. If a market begins to show declining occupancy or increased competition, investors can be alerted early and adjust strategy accordingly. This proactive approach reduces exposure to underperforming assets.

Another powerful concept introduced by AI is portfolio diversification within short-term rentals. Instead of relying on a single property or location, investors can use AI to evaluate multiple markets and compare performance potential across regions. This allows for strategic diversification, reducing risk while increasing overall income stability. AI can recommend expansion markets based on tourism growth, pricing strength, and occupancy trends, helping investors scale intelligently rather than randomly.

AI also supports hybrid strategies that combine fix and flip with short-term rental optimization. For example, a property initially intended for flipping may generate higher returns if converted into a short-term rental under certain market conditions. AI can compare both exit strategies—flip versus hold—and recommend the most profitable path based on real-time data. This flexibility allows investors to adapt to changing markets rather than committing to a single strategy prematurely. Financing and cash flow management are also enhanced through AI integration. Short-term rentals often require higher upfront investment for furnishing and setup, but can generate higher returns over time. AI helps investors model cash flow scenarios, including startup costs, operating expenses, and revenue projections, to determine break-even timelines and long-term profitability. This helps prevent undercapitalization and improves financial planning accuracy.

Ultimately, AI transforms short-term rental investing from a hands-on hospitality business into a structured, data-driven investment system. Instead of reacting to bookings, pricing changes, and guest behavior manually, investors operate within an automated ecosystem that continuously optimizes performance. This allows for higher efficiency, greater scalability, and more predictable income generation.

For investors already experienced in fix and flip strategies, short-term rentals represent a natural expansion opportunity. The same principles of acquisition, analysis, renovation, and exit still apply, but with added layers of real-time optimization and revenue management. AI becomes the bridge that connects these strategies into a unified real estate ecosystem capable of generating both short-term profits and long-term wealth.

"The Property That Became a Machine"

Daniel had always thought of himself as a fix and flip investor first. He liked the speed, the transformation, and the clear exit at the end of each project. Buy low, renovate, sell high—then move on. It was clean, predictable, and satisfying. But after several successful flips, he started noticing something: he was constantly starting over. Every deal reset the cycle. Every profit was temporary. He began wondering if there was a way to make properties work beyond a single transaction.

That's when he came across the idea of short-term rental investing.

At first, he dismissed it. It seemed complicated—too many variables, too many guest interactions, too much ongoing management. But the more he looked into it, the more he realized something important: the same properties he was flipping could potentially generate ongoing income if managed differently.

One of his recent flip properties was sitting on the market longer than expected. It was fully renovated, staged, and ready to sell, but buyer demand had slowed slightly due to rising interest rates. Offers were coming in lower than he wanted. Frustrated, Daniel decided to test something new.

He ran the property through an AI short-term rental analysis tool. Within seconds, the system generated a completely different perspective. Instead of focusing on resale value, it analyzed nightly rental rates, seasonal occupancy trends, and local tourism demand. It showed him projected monthly income that was significantly higher than expected. Even after factoring in management costs, cleaning, and utilities, the property had strong cash flow potential.

Daniel was surprised.

The same property that was struggling as a flip suddenly looked like a strong income-producing asset.

He decided to pause the sale and experiment.

The AI system helped him set up a full short-term rental strategy. It recommended pricing structures based on seasonal demand, suggested listing optimization changes, and even provided ideal occupancy targets. It also flagged peak tourism periods in the area that he had never considered.

Within a few weeks, the property was listed on a short-term rental platform.

The first bookings came quickly.

Then more followed.

What shocked Daniel wasn't just the income—it was the consistency. Instead of waiting for one buyer to purchase the property, he now had multiple guests generating revenue every week. The property was no longer a one-time transaction. It had become a continuous income engine.

But the real turning point came later.

One evening, Daniel reviewed the AI dashboard for the property. It showed occupancy forecasts, pricing adjustments, and revenue trends. It also suggested small changes—updating listing photos, adjusting minimum stay rules during peak weekends, and increasing pricing during local events.

He followed the recommendations.

Revenue increased almost immediately.

As weeks passed, Daniel realized something important. He wasn't managing a rental anymore. He was managing a system. The property was operating like a machine—adjusting pricing, optimizing bookings, and generating income with minimal intervention.

One day, while reviewing his portfolio, he noticed something even more surprising. Another property he had planned to flip was now being analyzed as a potential short-term rental instead. The AI system had flagged it as a higher long-term income asset than a quick flip.

For the first time, Daniel had to make a strategic choice: flip for one-time profit or hold for ongoing cash flow. He chose to hold.

Months later, that decision changed everything. His income was no longer dependent on buying and selling. It was coming from multiple streams of optimized rental properties working continuously in the background.

Daniel leaned back one evening and looked at his dashboard.

He realized something simple but powerful.

He hadn't just flipped a house into a rental.

He had turned a single property into a system that worked for him every single day.

And from that point forward, he stopped thinking like a flipper—and started thinking like someone building machines out of real estate.

Chapter 8

AI in Real Estate Financing and Loan Strategy Optimization

Financing is one of the most critical yet often misunderstood components of fix and flip investing. Many investors focus heavily on finding deals and managing renovations but treat financing as a secondary concern, simply choosing whatever loan is most readily available. In reality, financing structure directly impacts profitability, scalability, and risk exposure. A poorly structured loan can eliminate profit margins even on a well-executed flip, while an optimized financing strategy can significantly increase returns and allow investors to scale more efficiently. Artificial intelligence introduces a new level of precision into real estate financing by helping investors compare loan options, model cash flow impacts, and identify the most efficient capital structures for each deal.

AI-driven financing analysis begins with loan comparison. In traditional investing, borrowers often compare interest rates, points, and terms manually across a limited number of lenders. This process is time-consuming and often incomplete, leading investors to miss more favorable options. AI systems can instantly compare multiple financing products including hard money loans, DSCR loans, conventional financing, private lending, and HELOC-based strategies. Instead of focusing only on interest rates, AI evaluates the full cost of capital, including origination fees, prepayment penalties, draw schedules, and holding cost impacts. This creates a more complete financial picture of each financing option.

One of the most powerful applications of AI in financing is DSCR loan optimization. Debt Service Coverage Ratio (DSCR) loans are commonly used for investment properties, especially in rental or short-term rental strategies. AI can analyze projected rental income, operating expenses, and debt obligations to determine loan eligibility and optimal leverage levels. This allows investors to understand not only whether they qualify for a loan, but how much leverage they should use to maximize returns without increasing unnecessary risk. Instead of relying on lender assumptions alone, investors can simulate different DSCR scenarios to identify the most efficient borrowing structure.

AI also enhances fix and flip financing strategy by modeling the impact of loan terms on overall profitability. For example, short-term bridge loans often have higher interest rates but allow for faster acquisition and renovation cycles. AI can compare these costs against projected profits to determine whether a deal remains viable under different financing scenarios. It can also simulate holding cost increases if a project is delayed, helping investors understand how sensitive a deal is to timeline disruptions. This level of insight allows for more informed borrowing decisions before committing capital.

Another important aspect of AI in financing is capital stacking optimization. Many investors use multiple sources of capital to fund deals, including personal funds, credit lines, private lenders, and institutional loans. Managing these layers of capital can become complex, especially when multiple projects are active simultaneously. AI systems can optimize capital allocation by determining which funding sources should be used for each deal based on cost, speed, and risk. This ensures that high-cost capital is used only when necessary, while lower-cost capital is prioritized for longer-term investments.

Risk management is also significantly improved through AI-powered financing analysis. Every loan carries risk, but the level of risk varies depending on structure, leverage, and market conditions. AI can evaluate how changes in interest rates, property values, or holding times impact loan sustainability. It can also identify scenarios where over-leveraging could create cash flow stress or reduce exit flexibility. By modeling worst-case and best-case scenarios, investors gain a clearer understanding of financial exposure before committing to a deal. AI also supports refinancing strategy optimization. In many fix and flip or rental strategies, refinancing is used to extract equity or reduce debt costs after renovation or stabilization. AI can analyze optimal refinancing timing based on market conditions, property value appreciation, and interest rate trends. This helps investors decide when to refinance, how much equity to pull out, and which loan structure will provide the most long-term benefit. Instead of reacting to lender offers, investors can proactively plan refinancing strategies based on predictive data.

Another critical function of AI in financing is prequalification automation. Traditionally, loan qualification involves manual document review, credit checks, and lender back-and-forth communication. AI systems can streamline this process by analyzing borrower profiles, income patterns, credit data, and asset structures to determine eligibility across multiple loan products simultaneously. This speeds up prequalification and allows investors to focus only on financing options that are realistically available to them.

AI also improves leverage optimization, which is one of the most important factors in real estate profitability. While higher leverage can increase returns, it also increases risk exposure. AI helps investors find the optimal balance between leverage and safety by modeling different debt structures against projected cash flows and exit values. This allows investors to maximize returns without overexposing themselves to market volatility or interest rate fluctuations.

Another important benefit of AI financing systems is timing optimization. The timing of loan acquisition, rate locks, and refinancing decisions can significantly impact profitability. AI can analyze interest rate trends, lender appetite, and macroeconomic indicators to recommend optimal timing for securing financing. This ensures that investors are not locking in unfavorable terms during volatile market conditions and are instead positioning themselves strategically.

AI also enhances negotiation power with lenders. By understanding multiple financing options and simulated outcomes, investors can approach lenders with stronger data-backed positions. Instead of accepting standard terms, they can negotiate based on comparative analysis, risk profiles, and alternative funding structures identified by AI. This leads to more favorable loan terms and improved financial efficiency.

Ultimately, AI transforms real estate financing from a static decision into a dynamic optimization process. Instead of choosing the first available loan, investors evaluate financing as part of a larger system that includes acquisition, renovation, and exit strategy. Every financial decision becomes interconnected, allowing for more strategic planning and improved profitability. This chapter establishes financing as a core strategic pillar of AI-driven real estate investing. When combined with deal sourcing, property analysis, renovation management, and exit optimization, financing becomes part of a fully integrated system that maximizes efficiency and reduces risk across the entire investment lifecycle.

"The Loan That Changed His Strategy"

Michael had always thought of financing as something simple in real estate investing. You found a deal, you got a loan, you closed, and you moved forward. He rarely questioned the structure behind his loans. As long as the numbers worked on paper and the lender approved him quickly, he assumed it was the right decision. For years, this approach had worked well enough. He had completed several successful flips, made consistent profits, and built a steady rhythm in his business.

But everything changed when he started scaling.

As Michael began taking on more deals, financing became more complicated. Different lenders offered different terms. Some required higher down payments. Others had faster approvals but higher interest rates. A few offered attractive rates but came with strict repayment schedules that limited flexibility. Suddenly, financing was no longer a simple step—it was a decision that impacted every part of his business. One afternoon, Michael was reviewing two potential deals at the same time. Both properties looked profitable. Both had strong renovation upside. But the financing options were completely different. One lender offered a fast hard money loan with higher interest but quick closing. Another offered a lower-rate option but required more documentation and a longer approval timeline.

Michael felt stuck.

Choosing one meant giving up the benefits of the other. He started running spreadsheets, trying to compare scenarios manually, but the more he analyzed, the more unclear the decision became. Both options seemed viable, but neither felt clearly optimal.

Frustrated, he decided to try something new.

A colleague had recently introduced him to an AI financing analysis tool. Skeptical but curious, Michael entered both deals into the system along with the financing options. Within seconds, the AI generated a full comparison report.

What he saw immediately changed his perspective.

The system didn't just compare interest rates. It analyzed total cost of capital, holding time sensitivity, projected profit margins, and risk exposure under different timelines. One deal showed higher short-term profit but significantly higher risk if the renovation was delayed. The other showed slightly lower profit but far greater stability under multiple market scenarios.

Even more surprising, the AI recommended a hybrid financing approach Michael had not considered. It suggested using a short-term loan for acquisition and renovation, followed by a strategic refinance after stabilization to reduce overall cost of capital.

Michael stared at the screen.

He had never thought about combining financing strategies like that.

Instead of choosing blindly, he followed the AI's recommendation.

The results were immediate.

The project moved faster than expected due to streamlined funding. Renovation stayed on schedule. And when the refinance occurred, his long-term borrowing costs were significantly lower than his usual structure. The final profit on the deal was higher than anything he had achieved before—not because the property was better, but because the financing was smarter. A few weeks later, Michael reviewed his second deal using the same system. This time, the AI flagged a major issue he had completely overlooked. One financing option looked attractive on the surface, but when modeled against potential delays in renovation and slower resale conditions, it showed a high probability of reduced profitability or even breakeven outcomes.

Without the AI analysis, he likely would have chosen the wrong loan.

That realization hit him harder than he expected.

For the first time, Michael understood that financing wasn't just about getting money to close a deal. It was about structuring capital in a way that aligned with risk, timing, and long-term strategy.

Over the next few months, he began using AI for every financing decision. Instead of reacting to lender offers, he compared multiple scenarios before committing. Instead of focusing only on interest rates, he evaluated full capital efficiency. Instead of guessing, he modeled outcomes.

His entire approach to investing began to shift.

Deals that once felt risky now felt structured. Financing decisions that once caused stress now felt clear. And for the first time, Michael realized that the real difference between average investors and top performers wasn't just deal flow or renovation skill—it was how intelligently they structured their capital.

One evening, as he closed another profitable deal, Michael looked at his dashboard and thought back to how he used to make decisions.

Simple. Fast. But often incomplete.

Now everything was different.

He wasn't just borrowing money anymore.

He was designing financial systems that worked in his favor at every stage of the investment.

Chapter 9

AI Portfolio Management and Scaling Real Estate Operations

As investors progress beyond individual fix and flip deals and begin building multiple income-producing projects simultaneously, the complexity of managing their real estate business increases exponentially. What once felt manageable with one or two properties quickly becomes overwhelming when five, ten, or more projects are active at the same time. At this stage, success is no longer determined by deal selection alone, but by the ability to manage an entire portfolio efficiently, consistently, and strategically. Artificial intelligence becomes the central operating system that allows investors to scale beyond human limitations and transition from reactive project management to proactive portfolio control.

AI portfolio management begins with centralized visibility across all assets. In traditional real estate investing, investors often manage each property separately, tracking deals in spreadsheets, notes, or disconnected software systems. This fragmented approach makes it difficult to understand overall performance. AI changes this by consolidating all properties into a single intelligent dashboard that tracks acquisition costs, renovation progress, holding expenses, projected profits, and exit timelines in real time. Instead of looking at properties individually, investors can now see their entire portfolio as a unified system.

One of the most important advantages of AI in portfolio management is performance tracking and comparison. Not all properties perform equally, even if they follow similar strategies. AI systems analyze each deal based on return on investment, time to completion, renovation efficiency, and exit performance. This allows investors to identify which types of deals consistently perform best and which ones underperform. Over time, this data becomes extremely valuable because it reveals patterns that are not obvious when analyzing deals individually. Investors begin to understand which markets, property types, and strategies produce the highest returns.

AI also plays a critical role in capital allocation across a portfolio. As multiple projects run simultaneously, investors must decide where to focus resources such as time, money, and attention. Without structured systems, this often leads to imbalanced decision-making, where weaker deals consume too many resources while stronger deals are under-supported. AI solves this by ranking properties based on projected returns, risk levels, and capital efficiency. This allows investors to prioritize high-performing assets and strategically allocate resources where they generate the most impact. Another key function of AI in portfolio scaling is real-time risk monitoring. As the number of properties increases, so does exposure to risk. These risks may include market shifts, construction delays, budget overruns, or financing issues. AI continuously monitors all active projects and identifies early warning signals that may indicate future problems. For example, if multiple properties in a specific market begin showing slower sales velocity, the system can flag a potential market cooling trend. If contractor performance declines on one project, it can alert the investor before delays escalate across the portfolio.

AI also improves forecasting at the portfolio level. Instead of predicting outcomes for individual properties in isolation, AI systems analyze the entire portfolio to project total profit, cash flow, and timeline completion. This allows investors to understand not only how each deal performs, but how all deals interact together financially. This macro-level forecasting is critical for scaling because it helps investors make strategic decisions about reinvesting profits, acquiring new properties, or adjusting exit timelines based on overall portfolio performance.

Another major benefit of AI portfolio management is operational automation. As portfolios grow, administrative tasks such as tracking payments, monitoring contractors, updating budgets, and analyzing reports become increasingly time-consuming. AI reduces this burden by automating repetitive processes and generating structured updates across all properties. Instead of manually updating spreadsheets or checking individual project statuses, investors receive automated summaries that highlight key changes, risks, and opportunities across their entire portfolio.

AI also enhances diversification strategy within real estate portfolios. Many investors unintentionally concentrate too much capital in similar types of deals or markets, which increases vulnerability to market fluctuations. AI helps prevent this by analyzing portfolio composition and identifying imbalances. It can recommend diversification across different property types, geographic regions, or investment strategies such as flips, rentals, and short-term rentals. This creates a more stable portfolio that can withstand market changes more effectively.

Another important aspect of AI portfolio management is liquidity planning. Real estate investing often requires careful timing of cash inflows and outflows. AI systems can forecast when properties are expected to sell, when renovation costs will peak, and when capital will be tied up or released. This allows investors to plan financing strategies more effectively and avoid liquidity shortages that could stall future deals. By understanding cash flow timing across the entire portfolio, investors can maintain smoother operations and reduce financial stress.

AI also supports strategic scaling decisions. As portfolios grow, investors must decide when and how to expand. AI provides data-driven insights into scaling readiness by analyzing current performance, capital availability, and market conditions. It can recommend whether an investor is ready to increase deal volume, expand into new markets, or shift strategies based on portfolio stability. This prevents overextension and ensures that scaling happens in a controlled and sustainable manner.

Another critical advantage of AI is portfolio optimization over time. Real estate investing is not static; it evolves based on market cycles, interest rates, and economic conditions. AI continuously learns from portfolio performance and updates recommendations based on new data. This allows investors to refine their strategy over time, improving decision-making with each completed deal. The portfolio effectively becomes a learning system that grows smarter with experience.

Ultimately, AI transforms portfolio management from a manual, reactive process into a fully integrated, intelligent system. Instead of managing individual properties in isolation, investors operate within a structured ecosystem where every asset contributes to overall performance. This shift allows for greater scalability, improved efficiency, and more predictable long-term results.

Investors who embrace AI portfolio management are no longer limited by how many deals they can personally track or manage. Instead, they are limited only by the capacity of their systems. This is the defining difference between small-scale operators and large-scale real estate investors. One manages properties; the other manages systems that manage properties.

"When the Portfolio Started Thinking"

Evan had always been proud of his ability to stay organized. In the early years of his fix and flip career, he carefully managed every deal himself. He tracked budgets in spreadsheets, monitored renovation progress through daily calls with contractors, and personally reviewed every financial decision. It worked well when he had one or two projects at a time. But as his success grew, so did the complexity of his business.

At first, it felt exciting. More deals meant more income. More income meant more opportunity. But soon, Evan began to feel overwhelmed. He was juggling multiple flips at once, each at different stages of renovation, financing, and resale. One property needed urgent contractor attention, another was delayed due to permitting issues, and a third was approaching its listing date with uncertainty around pricing. Every day felt like triage. He wasn't building wealth anymore. He was managing chaos.

One evening, after reviewing updates from five different projects, Evan realized he couldn't clearly answer a simple question: "Which of my deals is actually performing the best right now?" He had spreadsheets, notes, and estimates—but no unified view of his portfolio. Everything was fragmented.

That night, he decided to try something different.

He had recently been introduced to an AI portfolio management system designed for real estate investors. Instead of tracking each property separately, the system consolidated all his active deals into one dashboard. Reluctantly, he uploaded his portfolio data.

Within minutes, everything changed.

For the first time, Evan saw all of his properties in one place. Each deal was ranked based on projected profitability, risk level, and timeline efficiency. One project was flagged as high-performing with strong upside potential. Another was marked as at-risk due to contractor delays. A third showed stable performance but limited upside compared to others in the portfolio.

Evan stared at the screen in silence. He had never seen his business this clearly before. The system didn't stop there. It began generating recommendations. It suggested reallocating contractor resources from a slower project to a higher-performing one. It flagged a property where holding costs were increasing faster than expected and recommended accelerating the listing timeline. It even identified a deal that, while profitable, was consuming too much capital relative to its return.

At first, Evan felt resistance. He was used to making these decisions himself. Trusting a system felt uncomfortable. But over the next few days, he began following the recommendations one by one.

The changes were immediate.

Delays were reduced because resources were redistributed more efficiently. Cash flow improved because underperforming assets were identified earlier. Stress decreased because he no longer had to manually track every detail. Instead of reacting to problems, he was now responding to structured insights.

One morning, Evan noticed something strange. He wasn't constantly checking updates anymore. The system was doing that for him. Instead of chasing information, he was receiving summaries that told him exactly what mattered.

His role had shifted. He was no longer managing individual properties.

He was managing a system that managed properties.

Months passed, and Evan's portfolio continued to grow. But something important had changed—growth no longer created chaos. It created structure. Each new deal plugged into the same system. Each new property added data that improved future decisions.

One afternoon, Evan reviewed his entire portfolio again. He noticed something remarkable. The system had begun to identify patterns in his business that he had never seen before. It showed which types of flips produced the highest returns, which contractors delivered the most consistent results, and which markets were becoming more or less favorable over time.

It wasn't just managing his portfolio anymore.

It was learning from it.

That realization hit him deeply.

He wasn't just building a real estate business anymore. He was building an evolving system that understood his business better than he did at the operational level.

And for the first time, Evan understood what real scaling meant. It wasn't about doing more deals.

It was about building something that could think, adapt, and improve without breaking under pressure.

Chapter 10

Advanced AI Real Estate Systems and Fully Automated Investing Businesses

At the highest level of real estate investing, the goal is no longer simply to find deals, flip properties, or even manage a portfolio efficiently. The ultimate evolution is the creation of a fully integrated, AI-driven real estate business that operates continuously, identifies opportunities automatically, evaluates them instantly, executes decisions efficiently, and improves over time without requiring constant manual intervention. This is the stage where real estate investing transitions from a hands-on profession into a structured, semi-autonomous system. Artificial intelligence becomes the core infrastructure that connects every phase of the business—from acquisition to analysis, renovation, financing, marketing, and exit—into a single operating engine.

Advanced AI real estate systems begin with full-cycle automation of deal flow. Instead of manually searching for properties or relying on inconsistent lead sources, investors can build systems that continuously scan the market for opportunities based on predefined criteria. These systems evaluate listings, off-market properties, tax records, and distressed assets in real time, filtering opportunities based on profitability thresholds, risk tolerance, and investment strategy. This creates a continuous pipeline of deals without requiring the investor to actively search for them. The business begins to generate opportunities as a function of its own system design.

Once deals are identified, AI systems immediately transition into evaluation mode. This includes automated analysis of ARV, renovation costs, holding expenses, financing structures, and exit strategy projections. Instead of manually reviewing each property, investors receive structured deal reports that include profit ranges, risk scores, and recommended actions. The decision-making process becomes significantly faster and more consistent, allowing investors to evaluate hundreds of opportunities in the time it would traditionally take to analyze a few.

At the core of advanced systems is predictive analytics. Unlike traditional investing, which is based on current data and historical trends, AI systems begin to forecast future conditions. This includes predicting neighborhood appreciation trends, identifying emerging investment hotspots, and forecasting changes in buyer demand. These predictive models allow investors to position themselves ahead of market shifts rather than reacting after changes have already occurred. This forward-looking capability is what separates basic automation from truly advanced AI investing systems.

Another key component is autonomous workflow execution. In a fully developed system, AI does not simply provide recommendations—it initiates actions based on predefined rules. For example, if a property meets specific profit criteria, the system can trigger outreach to sellers, generate offer templates, or schedule contractor assessments. If a renovation is delayed, it can automatically adjust timelines and update financial projections. This reduces the need for constant human input and allows the system to maintain momentum even when the investor is not actively engaged.

Advanced AI systems also integrate deeply with financing and capital management. Instead of treating financing as a separate step, the system continuously evaluates capital efficiency across all deals. It determines how funds should be allocated, when refinancing should occur, and how leverage should be optimized across the portfolio. This ensures that capital is always deployed in the most efficient way possible, maximizing returns while controlling risk exposure.

Marketing and exit execution are also fully integrated into advanced systems. Once a property reaches a certain stage in the investment cycle, AI automatically prepares listing materials, analyzes buyer demand, and determines optimal pricing strategies. It can adjust marketing strategies in real time based on engagement levels, ensuring that properties are positioned effectively in the market. This reduces time on market and increases the likelihood of achieving target profit margins.

Another defining feature of advanced AI systems is continuous learning and optimization. Every completed deal feeds data back into the system, improving future performance. The system learns which types of properties generate the highest returns, which renovation strategies are most effective, and which markets are most stable. Over time, this creates a compounding intelligence effect where the system becomes increasingly accurate and efficient with each transaction.

Risk management is also fully embedded into advanced systems. Instead of identifying risk after problems occur, AI continuously monitors portfolio exposure, market volatility, and project performance to detect early warning signals. If risk levels increase beyond acceptable thresholds, the system can recommend adjustments such as slowing acquisition activity, increasing liquidity reserves, or shifting investment focus to lower-risk opportunities. This proactive approach significantly reduces downside exposure.

At this stage, the investor's role shifts dramatically. Instead of manually managing deals, the investor becomes the architect of the system. Their focus is no longer on individual transactions, but on designing rules, refining strategies, and optimizing system performance. They determine investment criteria, risk tolerance, scaling limits, and capital allocation rules, while the AI system executes within those boundaries. This shift from operator to system designer is what enables true scalability.

Another important aspect of advanced AI real estate systems is multi-strategy integration. Instead of focusing on a single investment approach, such as fix and flip or rental investing, the system can manage multiple strategies simultaneously. It can allocate some properties to short-term flips, others to long-term rentals, and others to hybrid strategies based on market conditions. This creates a diversified, adaptive investment ecosystem capable of adjusting to changing environments.

Scalability at this level is no longer constrained by human bandwidth. Traditional real estate investing is limited by how many deals an individual can personally analyze and manage. In contrast, AI-driven systems can process thousands of opportunities simultaneously, manage multiple projects in parallel, and optimize performance across an entire portfolio in real time. This removes the traditional ceiling on growth and allows investors to scale far beyond conventional limits.

Ultimately, advanced AI real estate systems represent the final evolution of modern investing. They transform real estate from a manual, labor-intensive business into an intelligent, adaptive, and scalable system. Investors who reach this level are no longer dependent on individual effort to generate results. Instead, they operate businesses that are capable of continuously generating opportunities, optimizing performance, and improving over time.

This chapter represents the culmination of the entire framework. Every concept from deal sourcing, property analysis, renovation management, financing, exit strategy, and portfolio scaling converges into one unified idea: building a real estate business that functions as an intelligent system rather than a collection of manual processes. This is the future of investing, where success is determined not by effort alone, but by the sophistication of the systems you build.

"The System That Never Slept"

Nathan had been in real estate long enough to remember what it felt like to do everything manually. In the early years, he worked constantly. He drove neighborhoods, analyzed listings late at night, called contractors during lunch breaks, and managed deals through endless spreadsheets. At the time, he believed this level of effort was necessary to succeed. Hard work was the system. Or at least, that's what he thought. As his business grew, so did the complexity. More deals meant more problems. More properties meant more decisions. Eventually, Nathan reached a point where he wasn't just working in his business—he was trapped inside it. Every day felt like reacting to something urgent. Every week felt like catching up. Every month felt like trying to regain control.

One night, after reviewing yet another series of delayed projects and compressed profit margins, Nathan sat alone in his office and asked himself a question he had avoided for years: "What would happen if I stopped managing everything myself?"

That question led him to something new.

He had recently been introduced to an advanced AI real estate system designed to manage entire investment portfolios autonomously. Unlike traditional tools that simply provided data, this system was designed to operate as an integrated business engine. It could source deals, analyze properties, manage renovations, optimize financing, and even execute exit strategies with minimal input.

Skeptical but exhausted, Nathan decided to test it.

He connected his entire portfolio to the system.

At first, nothing felt different. But within hours, he began to notice changes. New deal opportunities were being ranked automatically. Underperforming properties were flagged with clear recommendations. Renovation timelines were being adjusted based on contractor performance patterns. Financing structures were being optimized without his involvement.

For the first time in years, Nathan wasn't manually controlling every decision.

The system was handling it.

Days turned into weeks, and something unexpected happened. Instead of chaos increasing, things became more organized. Deals moved faster. Renovations stayed on track. Financial projections became clearer. He wasn't reacting to problems anymore because the system was identifying them before they escalated.

One morning, Nathan logged into his dashboard and saw something he didn't expect. The system had not only managed his portfolio—it had expanded it. It had identified new opportunities, filtered them based on his investment criteria, and prepared acquisition recommendations without him requesting it.

It wasn't just managing his business.

It was growing it.

Nathan sat back in silence. For years, he believed scaling meant doing more. More calls. More deals. More stress. But now he was beginning to understand something different. Real scaling wasn't about doing more work. It was about building something that could operate without being constantly pushed.

Over time, Nathan shifted his role completely. He stopped making daily operational decisions. Instead, he focused on adjusting system parameters—defining risk levels, refining acquisition criteria, and reviewing overall performance trends. The system handled execution. He handled direction.

One evening, he looked at his portfolio and realized something powerful. He no longer knew every detail of every deal—and he didn't need to. The system knew. It tracked everything, optimized everything, and learned from everything.

And it never stopped working.

Even when he wasn't logged in, deals were being analyzed. Markets were being scanned. Renovation updates were being processed. Opportunities were being ranked.

It didn't sleep.

It didn't pause.

It didn't forget.

Nathan closed his laptop and leaned back. For the first time in his entire career, he wasn't running a real estate business.

He had built something that ran itself.

And that changed everything.

Final Comments

The Future of AI in Real Estate Investing

Reaching the end of this series is not an endpoint in your journey as a real estate investor—it is the beginning of a fundamentally different way of operating in the world of property investing. What you have explored throughout these chapters is not just a set of strategies or tools, but a complete transformation in how real estate investing can be structured, executed, and scaled. Artificial intelligence is not a temporary enhancement or a passing trend. It is a foundational shift in how decisions are made, how opportunities are identified, and how businesses are built. The investors who understand this shift early are the ones who will define the next generation of real estate wealth creation.

For decades, real estate investing has been driven by human effort, experience, and intuition. Investors succeeded by learning markets over time, building relationships, and developing personal systems for analyzing deals. While those principles still matter, they are no longer sufficient on their own in a market that is becoming increasingly data-driven, competitive, and fast-moving. The introduction of AI does not remove the need for human judgment, but it dramatically enhances it. It allows investors to see further, move faster, and make decisions with greater clarity than ever before. What once took days of analysis can now be accomplished in seconds. What once required guesswork can now be supported by structured, predictive data.

One of the most important takeaways from this series is that AI is not a single tool—it is an ecosystem. It connects every part of the real estate investing process into a unified system. Deal sourcing, property analysis, renovation management, financing strategy, exit optimization, and portfolio scaling are no longer separate activities. They are interconnected components of a larger intelligent framework. When these components work together, the result is not just improved efficiency, but exponential capability. Investors are no longer limited by their individual capacity to process information or manage tasks. Instead, they are supported by systems that continuously analyze, optimize, and improve performance across every stage of the investment cycle.

Another key insight is the shift from reactive investing to proactive system design. Traditional investing often involves reacting to opportunities as they appear. A deal is found, analyzed, purchased, renovated, and sold. AI-driven investing changes this by introducing anticipation and prediction into the process. Instead of waiting for opportunities, investors build systems that identify them automatically. Instead of reacting to problems during renovations, investors receive early warnings and optimization suggestions. Instead of guessing market timing for exits, investors rely on predictive models that analyze demand, pricing behavior, and buyer activity in real time. This shift fundamentally changes the role of the investor from operator to system architect.

As investors begin to adopt these systems, they often experience a transformation in how they view time and effort. In traditional real estate investing, success is often directly tied to personal effort. The more deals you analyze, the more calls you make, and the more time you invest, the greater your potential outcomes. However, AI introduces a different relationship between effort and results. Once systems are properly designed and implemented, they begin to operate continuously, generating insights, identifying opportunities, and optimizing decisions without constant manual input. This creates a separation between time spent and value created, allowing investors to focus more on strategy and less on execution.

This does not mean that human involvement becomes irrelevant. On the contrary, human judgment becomes even more important at a higher level. The role of the investor evolves into system design, oversight, and strategic refinement. Decisions are no longer made at the micro level of individual tasks but at the macro level of system behavior. Investors define rules, set parameters, evaluate performance trends, and adjust strategies based on system feedback. In this model, the investor becomes the decision-maker behind the system rather than the executor within it.

Another major transformation introduced through AI is the concept of compounding intelligence. In traditional investing, experience accumulates linearly. Each deal teaches lessons, but those lessons are often stored informally in memory or scattered across notes and spreadsheets. In an AI-driven system, every transaction becomes structured data that feeds back into the system. This means that each deal improves the accuracy of future analysis, each renovation improves cost estimation models, and each exit improves pricing and timing predictions. Over time, the system becomes more intelligent, more precise, and more efficient. This compounding effect creates a significant long-term advantage for investors who consistently use and refine AI systems.

It is also important to recognize that the future of real estate investing will not be defined by tools alone, but by how those tools are integrated into business models. Simply using AI for isolated tasks is not enough to create a competitive advantage. The real power comes from building integrated systems where AI supports every stage of the investment lifecycle. Investors who understand how to connect deal sourcing, analysis, renovation management, financing, and exit strategy into one cohesive system will be significantly ahead of those who continue operating in fragmented processes.

As this transformation continues, the gap between traditional investors and AI-enabled investors will widen. Those who rely solely on manual methods will find themselves competing in a market where speed, accuracy, and data-driven decision-making are increasingly essential. Meanwhile, those who embrace AI will be able to evaluate more deals, reduce risk more effectively, and scale their operations beyond previous limitations. This is not simply an improvement in efficiency—it is a structural shift in competitive advantage.

However, it is important to approach this evolution with balance and clarity. AI is a powerful tool, but it is not a replacement for experience, judgment, or accountability. Real estate investing still involves real-world variables such as contractors, markets, financing institutions, and human behavior. AI enhances decision-making, but it does not eliminate responsibility. The most successful investors will be those who learn how to combine technological intelligence with practical experience, using each to strengthen the other.

Looking forward, the future of real estate investing will likely become even more automated, predictive, and integrated. Systems will become more advanced in identifying opportunities before they reach the market, more precise in estimating costs and returns, and more adaptive to changing economic conditions. Investors who begin building these systems now are positioning themselves at the forefront of this evolution. Those who delay may find themselves operating in a market that has already moved beyond traditional methods.

Ultimately, this series has been about one central idea: real estate investing is evolving from a manual profession into an intelligent system-based industry. The investors who succeed in the future will not necessarily be those who work the hardest, but those who build the most effective systems. Artificial intelligence is the foundation of this shift, enabling investors to scale, optimize, and evolve in ways that were previously impossible.

As you move forward beyond this book, the most important action is not simply to learn the concepts, but to apply them. Systems only create value when they are implemented. Data only becomes powerful when it is used to make decisions. And AI only transforms investing when it is integrated into real business operations. The opportunity in front of you is not theoretical—it is practical, immediate, and scalable. The future of real estate investing is not coming—it is already here. The only question that remains is how quickly you choose to step into it.

www.ingramcontent.com/pod-product-compliance
Ingram Content Group UK Ltd.
Pitfield, Milton Keynes, MK11 3LW, UK
UKHW010012031026
15589UKWH00008B/1618

9 798295 885211